MOSQUITO BITE

ALEXANDRA SIY & DENNIS KUNKEL

ini Charlesbridge

To Rory, Hope, Leo, and Sky—A. S.

To my nieces Emily, Abby, and Olivia—D. K.

Thanks to Chris Porter of Chris Porter Illustration for colorizations of Dennis Kunkel's electron micrographs; Scott Campbell, laboratory director at the Arthropod-Borne Disease Laboratory, Suffolk County Department of Health Services, New York, for providing samples of the male *Culex* mosquitoes; Kelly Middleton, education specialist at San Gabriel Valley Mosquito and Vector Control District, California, for providing samples of *Culex* egg rafts and mosquitoes.

Special thanks to the children who were photographed while playing hide-and-seek and to their parents, especially Paige Rebeor.

Thanks to Yolanda LeRoy, our superb editor, and designer Susan Sherman, for her creative approach. Finally, we are most grateful to Eric Siy and Nancy Eckmann, our life collaborators, for their patience, support, good humor, and love.

First paperback edition 2005
Text and black-and-white photographs copyright © 2005 by Alexandra Siy
Photomicrographs copyright © 2005 by Dennis Kunkel

Published by Charlesbridge
85 Main Street
Watertown, MA 02472
(617) 926-0329
www.charlesbridge.com

Library of Congress Cataloging-in-Publication Data
Siy, Alexandra.
   Mosquito bite / Alexandra Siy; Dennis Kunkel.
      p. cm.
   ISBN 978-1-57091-591-8 (reinforced for library use)
   ISBN 978-1-57091-592-5 (softcover)
   ISBN 978-1-60734-146-8 (ebook pdf)
1. Culex pipiens—Life cycles—Juvenile literature. 2. Culex pipiens—Pictorial works—Juvenile literature.
3. Photomicrography—Juvenile literature. I. Kunkel, Dennis, ill. II. Title.
QL536.S54 2005
595.77'2—dc22   2004018959

Printed in Korea
(hc) 10 9 8 7 6 5 4 3
(sc) 10 9 8 7 6

Display type set in Roger, designed by Dave Berlow, The Font Bureau; text type set in Goudy;
   caption font set in Allspeed Italic, designed by David Bergsland and Quetzalcoatl
Printed by Sung In Printing in Gunpo-Si, Kyonggi-Do, Korea
Production supervision by Brian G. Walker; designed by Susan M. Sherman

"READY-OR-NOT-HERE-I-COME!"

The girl's voice calls out over the pulsing hum of crickets as she uncovers her eyes. It's a humid summer night. The rising moon casts just enough light for the boy to see her running across the grass.

The surface of a blade of grass is covered with spines and hair.

x200

3

The symbol x at the bottom of each micrograph indicates magnification. "x200" means that the object in the picture is two hundred times larger than life.

He's crouched like a cat behind the big, old tractor tire that used to be a swing—before the rope rotted and fell from the branch of the oak tree.

He listens. He hears the girl's footsteps near the garden, on the driveway, now by the flowers along the walk.

She's getting closer.

Suddenly, there's another sound. A droning buzz.

The boy's hand flutters across his face and brushes the back of his neck.

Something else is looking for the boy.

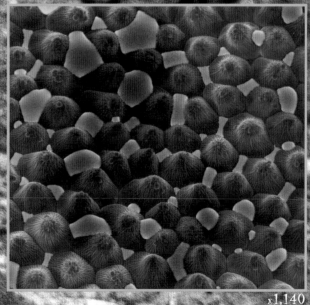

This rose petal is splashed with dewdrops.

x1,140

5

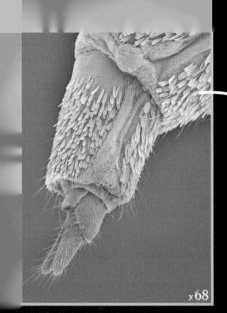

x68

The female *Culex* releases her eggs from a structure at the tip of her abdomen called an ovipositor.

Culex pipiens is the scientific name for the common house mosquito.

wings

abdomen

thorax

head

eye

palps →

legs

proboscis

antenna

x18

A mosquito wing has feathery scales along its edges and veins, and hairs called setae on its surface.

x330

6

The tubes that form *Culex's* compound eyes are each capped with a rounded lens.

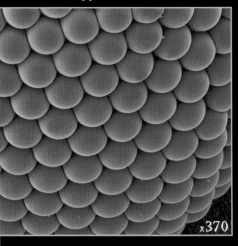

x370

Her name is *Culex pipiens*. Bordered with scales, her wings whine, beating about 500 times in one second. Her antennae, feathery and fine, detect the boy's breath. Her compound eyes guide her toward the boy's moving hand.

She's getting closer.

But this is not a playful game of hide-and-seek. *Culex* carries hundreds of tiny eggs inside her body. Finding the boy is a matter of life and death.

x145

This is a female mosquito antenna. *Culex's* two antennae detect carbon dioxide, odors, heat, and humidity—all signals that lead her to blood.

7

Culex is a very young mosquito, yet already she's lived a dangerous and complicated life.

She started out as a tiny egg laid on the surface of the rainwater trapped inside the rim of the old tire.

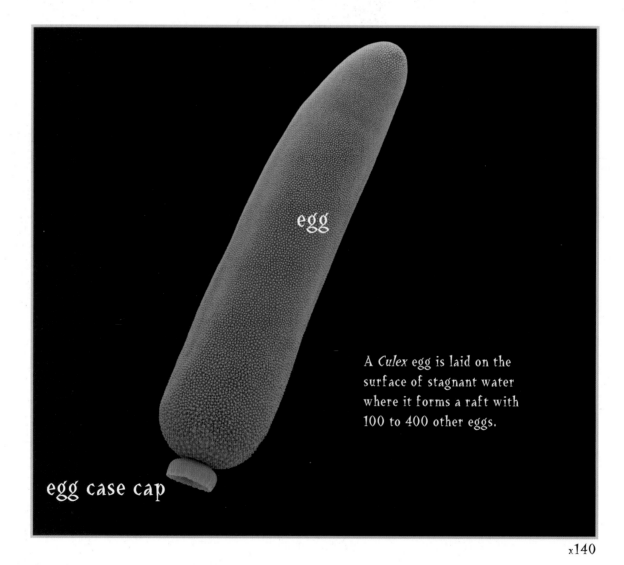

egg

egg case cap

A *Culex* egg is laid on the surface of stagnant water where it forms a raft with 100 to 400 other eggs.

x140

Attached to hundreds of other eggs, she floated within an egg raft that was no bigger than half a grain of rice.

Part of an egg raft with hatching larvae.

egg cases

egg case cap

mouth brushes

developing eye

x115

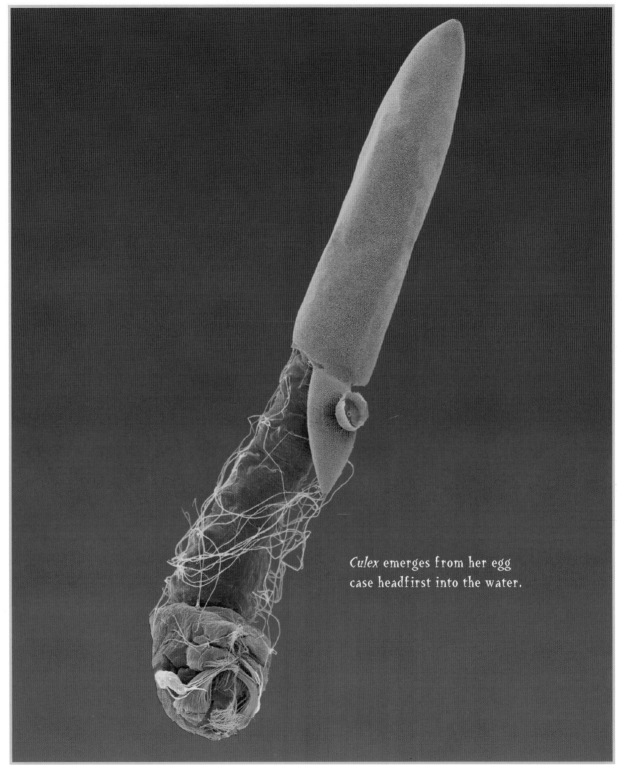

Culex emerges from her egg case headfirst into the water.

10

x130

Two days later all the eggs hatched. *Culex* burst out of her shell—a long, wiggling worm. She had big eyes and a hairy head that hung down into the water. She breathed through a tube in her tail, called a siphon.

water level

siphon

segmented abdomen

A larva's undeveloped eyes are called ocelli (singular = ocellus).

Culex's mouth brushes sweep food particles into her mouth.

mouth brushes

ocellus

x22

Culex feeds on plankton such as diatoms, which are single-celled algae with silica shells (shown in pink), and bacteria (orange rods). Some types of rod-shaped bacteria are deadly to mosquito larvae.

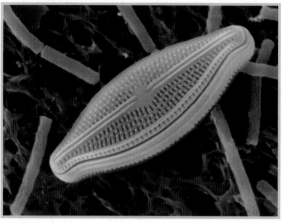

x1,830

For one week *Culex* fed on tiny creatures that also lived in the water. Day and night her waving whiskers swept the microscopic food into her open mouth.

All of *Culex*'s brothers and sisters fed in this manner, but not all of them lived. Some died from eating bacteria that cause disease. *Culex* was lucky. She survived and grew until she was three times her original size.

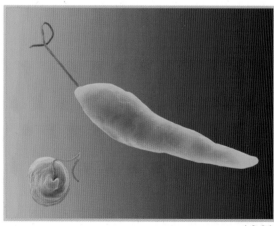

Euglena gracilis are another kind of plankton. They swim by whipping their thread-like flagellum.

x4,280

12

Some plankton, such as *Cyanobacteria*, live near the water's surface. They use energy from sunlight to produce food in a process called photosynthesis.

x1,955

These are other types of diatoms.

x2,455

breathing trumpets

cephalothorax
The cephalothorax develops
into both the head and thorax.

developing
eye

The abdomen flexes up and
down, propelling the pupa
through the water.

segmented abdomen

paddles
A pair of paddles is used to
move the pupa forward.

x29

Then she changed.

At twelve days old, her wormy body lost its soft skin and formed a new, hard outer covering. Now a pupa, *Culex* couldn't eat because she didn't have a mouth.

For a couple of days, *Culex* floated in the water. Sometimes she tumbled away from a hungry beetle whose movement she detected with her big eyes.

Beneath her shell she was changing again.

The adult *Culex* swallows air, inflating her soft body until it expands through the pupal covering. She must rest for several hours until her wings, legs, and body harden.

x15

On a hazy, muggy morning, *Culex* stretched, her pupal covering split open, and her new adult body unfolded. Gracefully, she stepped onto the water's surface. Then she flew up to a shaded branch of the oak tree to rest.

wings

abdomen

thorax

A male *Culex pipiens* finds his mate in a swarm of mosquitoes by detecting the female's flight tone: the buzzing sound made by her wings.

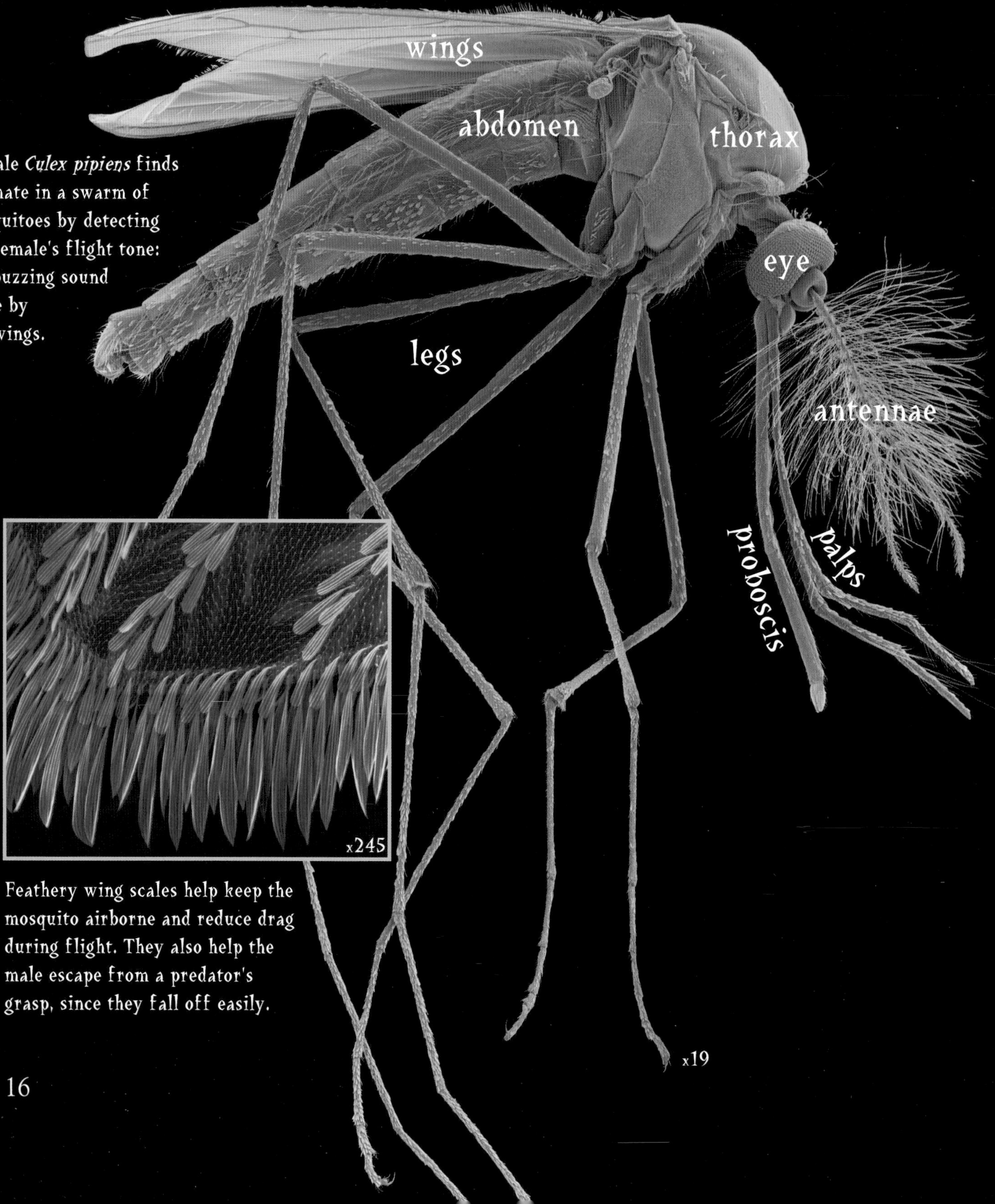

eye

antennae

legs

proboscis

palps

x245

Feathery wing scales help keep the mosquito airborne and reduce drag during flight. They also help the male escape from a predator's grasp, since they fall off easily.

x19

Two days later, in the red glow of the morning sky, *Culex* flew into a noisy cloud of male mosquitoes hovering above the garden.

Suddenly, a dragonfly raided the swarm. It caught a male with its front legs and devoured it immediately. As *Culex* veered away from the fray, the dragonfly's flashing blue-green wings clipped one of her legs—a minor injury because mosquitoes can balance on just five legs.

Soon after the attack, *Culex* and a male mosquito drifted to the ground in an insect hug. They mated.

Culex was ready for her main purpose in life: to make more mosquitoes.

x485

A male's antenna contains hundreds of sensitive hairs that vibrate in response to the female's buzz. The pair of antennae can locate a flying female with great accuracy.

17

Culex zooms through the night seeking the blood she needs to nourish the eggs inside her body. She's not thinking about where she will look or how she will hide. Her tiny brain is not capable of thought. Instead, she focuses her senses on finding her victim.

Culex detects a plume of carbon dioxide in the distance. Her wings whiz and whine as she zigzags closer.

The boy squirms behind the tire. *Culex* senses his movements with her eyes.

The girl stops. She listens. The boy freezes, holding his breath.

Culex feels heat. It's coming from the boy's sweaty neck.

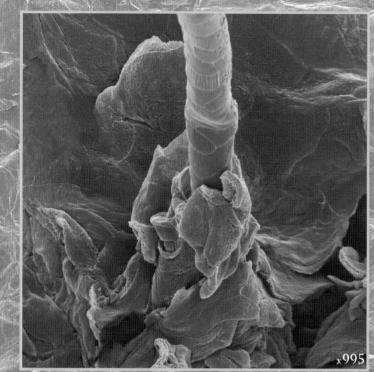

A human hair grows through the epidermis, or thin outer layer of human skin that is formed from layers of flat, dead cells.

x995

A human capillary, the smallest of all blood vessels, carries red blood cells through the dermis, the thick inner layer of skin. The dermis also includes nerves and sweat glands.

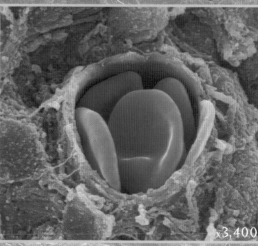

Female mosquitoes detect heat, moisture, and odors coming from exposed skin (shown here).
x77

x3,400

eye

antenna

antenna

palps

proboscis

labial sheath

labial sheath

knives

cutter

cutter

x 465

Culex feeds with the part of her mouth called the proboscis. Inside the proboscis is a pair of flexible serrated cutters that slide up and down alongside another pair of carving knives that slice through inner layers of skin.

A long pair of tubes is also found in the proboscis: one drips saliva into the wound, which keeps the blood flowing; the other is a straw for sucking in blood.

Culex is very close. She lands. She is so light the boy feels nothing. *Culex* pushes the tip of her mouth through the boy's skin. Her mouth is a bundle of long tubes and cutters that slide side by side like tiny knives.

The boy feels nothing.

Keeping her mouth in the hole, *Culex* stabs. With each poke, she pumps saliva from a tiny tube in her mouth. The saliva contains a chemical that will keep the blood flowing . . . if she ever finds it.

The boy feels nothing.

Finally, after fourteen stabs, *Culex* nicks a blood vessel. She tastes the blood. She immediately sucks a drop into her miniature straw. Now the blood is flowing, drop by drop, into her stomach.

Still the boy feels nothing.

Culex's belly swells. She is full.

At last the boy feels it: a mosquito bite!
As *Culex* struggles to lift her bloated body
into the thick night air, the boy smacks the back
of his neck.

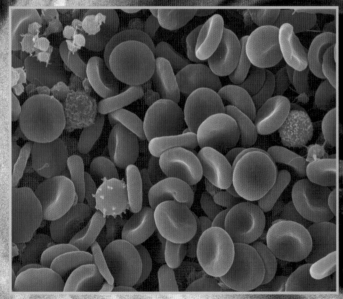

x1,530

Human blood contains red
blood cells (red) for carrying
oxygen, white blood cells
(green and purple) for
fighting infection, and
platelets (brown) for clotting.

"Found you!" shouts the girl. "Now you're 'it.' "

"And it's *your* turn to hide," says the boy.

Culex clings to the side of the big oak tree. Pink liquid containing the waste left over from her meal trickles from her body. It drips for almost an hour before *Culex* is light enough to fly.

That night in bed the boy scratches the itchy, hard, red lump that has appeared on the back of his neck. Hidden in darkness outside, *Culex* rests.

Tomorrow—and the next day, and the day after that—it will be *Culex*'s turn to hide. Spiders, insects, bats, and birds will hunt her until she is ready to lay her eggs . . .

Flakes of dead skin (green)
are tangled in the cotton
fibers (blue) of the T-shirt.

x150

25

. . . on the surface of the rainwater trapped in the rim of the big, old tractor tire that used to be a swing—before the rope rotted and fell from the branch of the oak tree.

More About Mosquitoes

Mosquitoes lived amid the dinosaurs, feeding off their blood. Today *Culex pipiens* (the scientific name for the common house mosquito) prefers bird blood but also feeds on human blood. *Culex* thrives worldwide, wherever there is dirty, stagnant water and a blood supply.

Culex pipiens is just one of more than 2,700 mosquito species. Mosquitoes are found on every continent except Antarctica.

All mosquitoes need water in which to lay their eggs. Ponds, puddles, ditches, birdbaths, barrels, tree holes, and old tires provide a place for mosquito eggs to hatch and the larvae to grow.

Like butterflies, most mosquitoes feed on flower nectar and plant juices. Only the females of some species feed on blood to nourish their eggs. Fewer still feed mainly on human blood. Yet just one bite from an infected mosquito can cause illness. Although its name simply means "little fly" in Spanish, the mosquito is the deadliest animal on Earth.

Culex's Life Cycle

EGG: 1–2 days

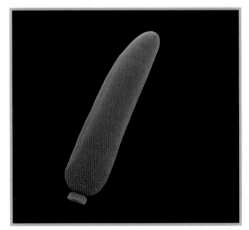

x54

WIGGLER (larva): 7–14 days

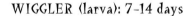

x9

28

Malaria, a disease transmitted primarily by the mosquito *Anopheles gambiae*, kills about two million people (mainly children in Africa) each year. Although scientists continue to seek new medicines to treat and prevent malaria, many experts think the cheapest and most effective means of preventing malarial infection is through the careful use of the controversial and widely banned pesticide DDT. Sprayed indoors on the walls of houses, DDT kills mosquitoes that would otherwise bite people as they sleep.

In the United States, where West Nile virus is a growing problem, people can protect themselves by knowing the habits of *Culex pipiens*. *Culex* is a night feeder and lays its eggs in stagnant water. Clearing clogged rain gutters and removing birdbaths, old cans, abandoned wading pools, and used tires help eliminate *Culex*'s breeding grounds. Window screens help protect people while they sleep. Wearing long sleeves and pants when outside at night limits the amount of exposed skin. Insect repellents containing safe amounts of DEET can be used to keep mosquitoes away. A thick layer of mineral oil or citronella also repels mosquitoes if applied frequently.

TUMBLER (pupa): 2-4 days

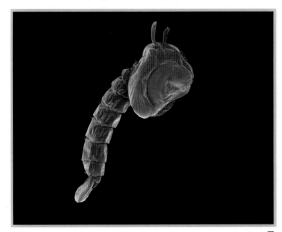

x7

ADULT: Can live several days, long enough to mate and lay eggs. Some adults live about a month, which is long enough to lay 3 or 4 egg rafts. A few hibernate over the winter (3-6 months) in garages, sheds, and basements. They resume feeding, mating, and egg laying in the spring.

life-size *Culex*

About the Micrographs

The color photographs in this book are called photomicrographs because they were taken with a scanning electron microscope (SEM). The SEM magnifies subjects from about 10 to 300,000 times. Unlike light microscopes, which have glass lenses and use visible white light to magnify a subject, electron microscopes have electromagnetic lenses and electrons. Electrons are invisible, high-energy subatomic particles. Compared to visible light wavelengths, electrons have a shorter wavelength and produce greater detail and higher magnification.

Because electrons are not within the visible light spectrum, SEM photographs are first produced as black-and-white images. A computer program is used to add colors to the subject, making it possible to highlight interesting features. Shown here is the original black-and-white photograph of a *Culex* head and forelegs. Two different colored versions of the same original image highlight the various body features. The colors used do not show the true colors of the *Culex* mosquito—just as all of the colored photographs in this book have been artistically rendered.

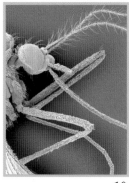
x10

x10

x10

30

Glossary

abdomen: The long, segmented part of an insect's body, located behind the thorax and head.

antennae: Two long, thin sensory organs located on the front of an insect's head.

aquatic: Living in water.

bacteria: A group of microscopic, one-celled living things.

capillary: The smallest kind of blood vessel.

cephalothorax: A body part consisting of a head and thorax joined together.

compound eye: An eye made of many lenses.

dermis: The thick inner layer of skin.

diatom: A single-celled alga with a silica shell.

epidermis: The protective outer layer of skin.

insect: A class of invertebrates with three main body parts: a head (with eyes, antennae, and mouth parts), a thorax (with six legs and usually two pairs of wings; mosquitoes have one pair), and a segmented abdomen.

larva: The immature form of an animal (such as an insect, invertebrate, amphibian, or fish) that does not look like the adult.

ocelli: The small simple eyes or eyespots of an invertebrate.

ovipositor: The pointed organ in female insects that lays eggs.

palps: The pair of small feelers that are part of the mouths of most insects.

photosynthesis: The process by which energy from sunlight is used to convert carbon dioxide and water into food (glucose).

plankton: Microscopic living things that float or swim in water.

proboscis: The long tube through which some insects suck liquid food.

pupa: The inactive form of an animal between the larval and adult stages.

setae: The hairs on the surface of a mosquito's wing.

siphon: The snorkle-like breathing tube on the tail end of a mosquito larva that comes in contact with the air.

thorax: The middle section of an insect body that bears the legs and wings.

Index

Resources

Centers for Disease Control and Prevention
http://www.cdc.gov/ncidod/dvbid/westnile
Learn more about West Nile virus.

Dennis Kunkel's website
http://education.denniskunkel.com
Browse the image library, use the interactive features, and find additional information about microscopy.

Florida State University
http://www.microscopy.fsu.edu
Experience a virtual scanning electron microscope (SEM). Click on "microscopy primer," then "virtual microscopy," then "scanning electron microscopy."

Iowa State University
http://www.mse.iastate.edu/microscopy/home.html
Learn how a scanning electron microscope (SEM) works and view student photomicrographs.

Kramer, Stephen. *Hidden Worlds: Looking Through a Scientist's Microscope*. Boston: Houghton Mifflin Company, 2001.

Nikon International Small World Competition
http://www.nikonsmallworld.com
View hundreds of award-winning photomicrographs.

Tomb, Howard. *MicroAliens: Dazzling Journeys with an Electron Microscope*. New York: Farrar, Straus & Giroux, 1993.

Walker, Richard. *Microscopic Life*. Boston: Kingfisher, 2004.